MAZE

FOR KIDS

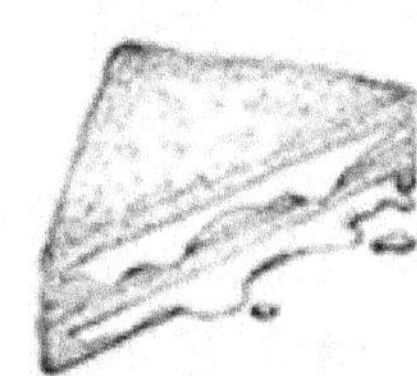

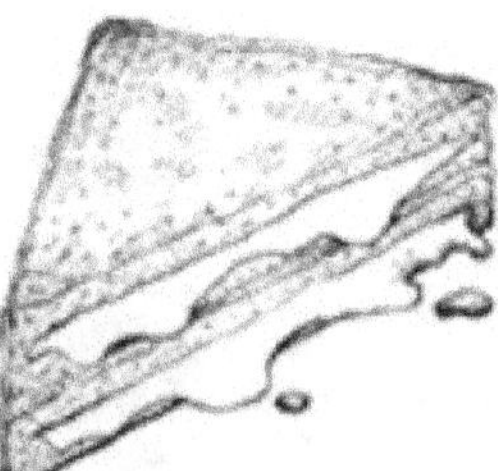

MAZE BOOK

SOCIAL MEDIA

- (f) /MySweetBooks1
- (t) /MySweetBooks1
- (i) /MySweetBooks1
- (p) /MySweetBooks

Email Us : mysweetbooks1@gmail.com

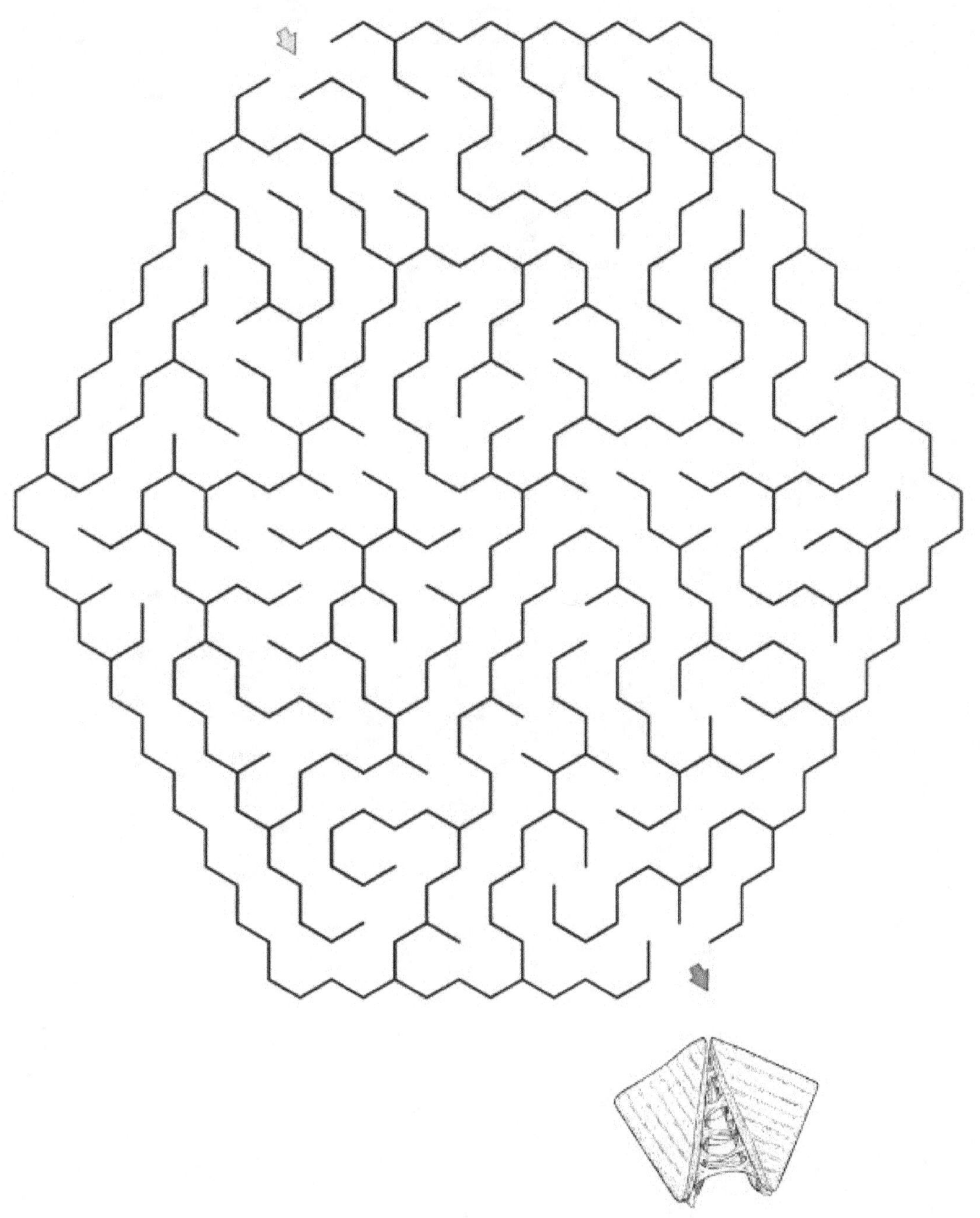

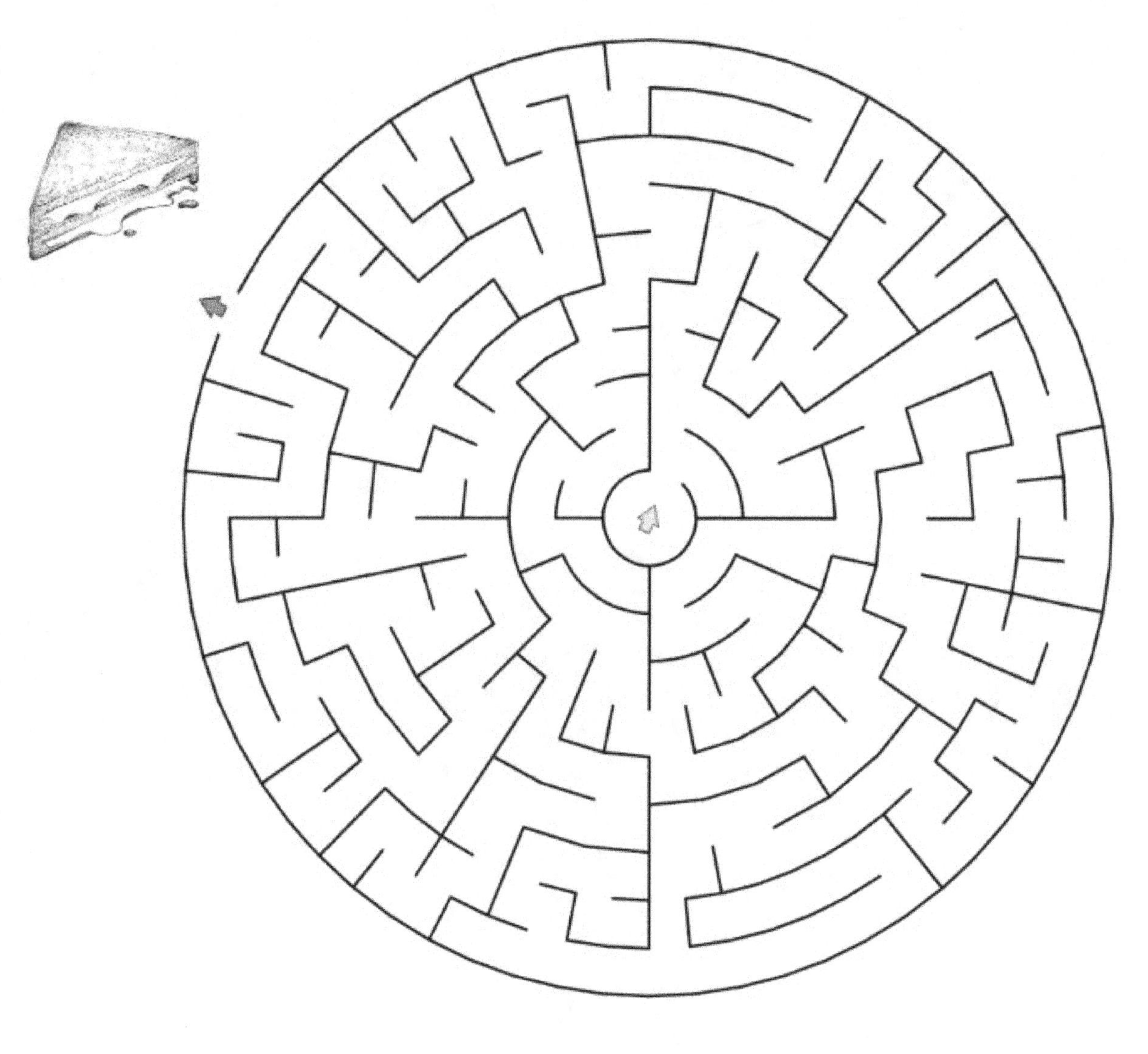

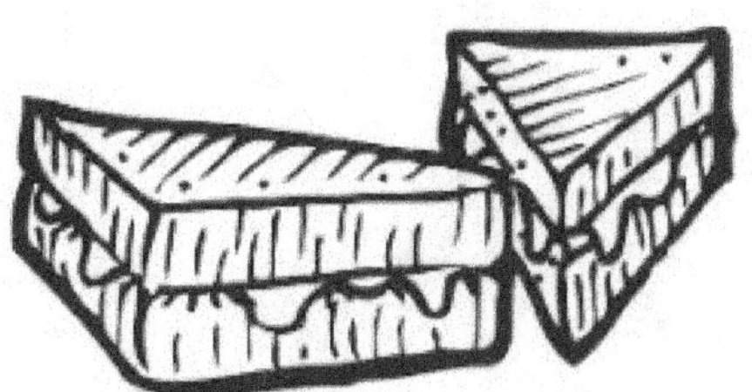

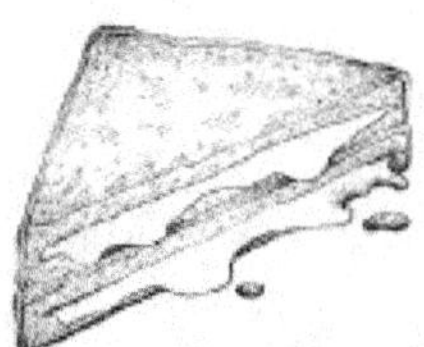

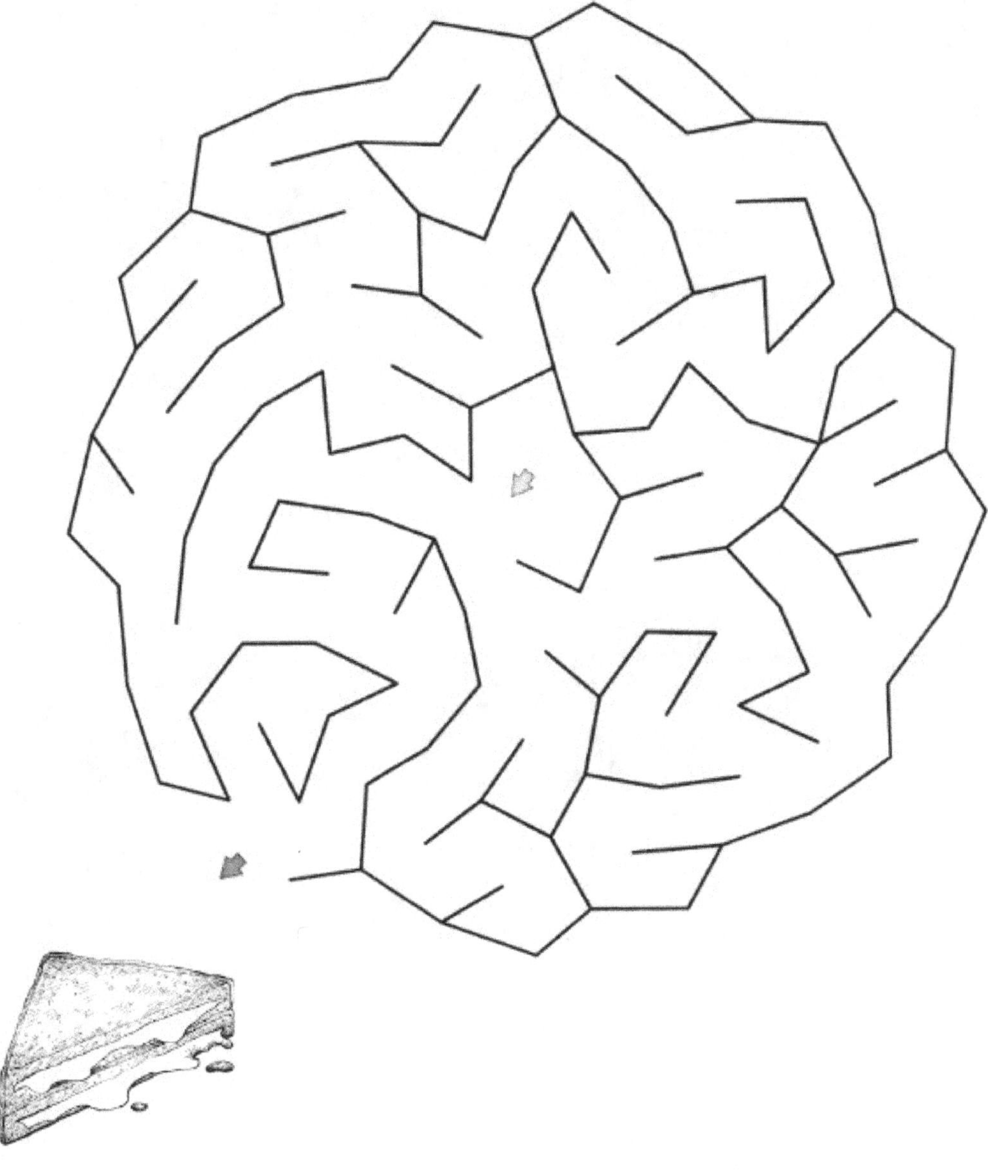

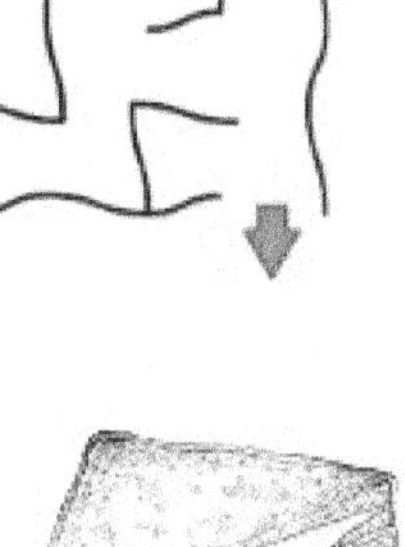

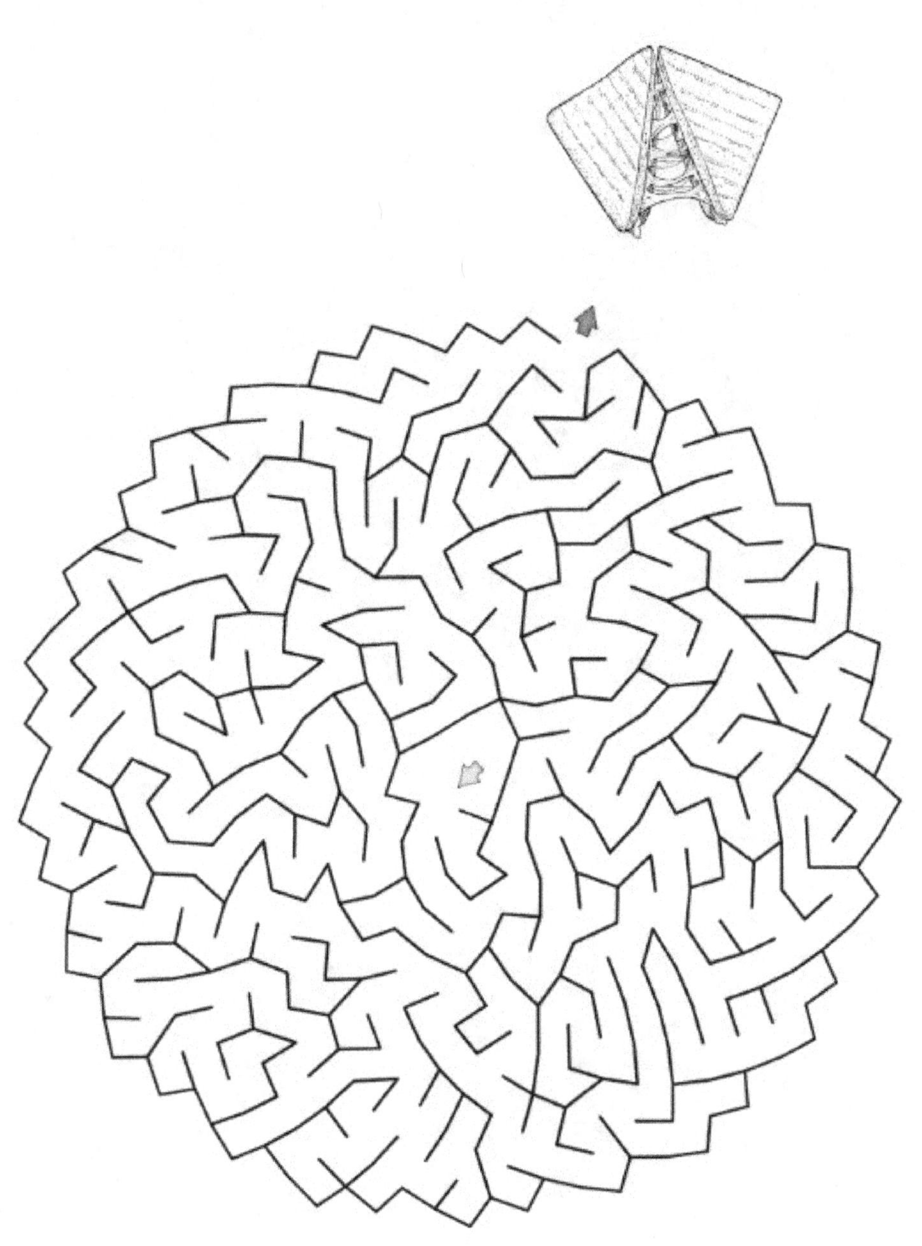

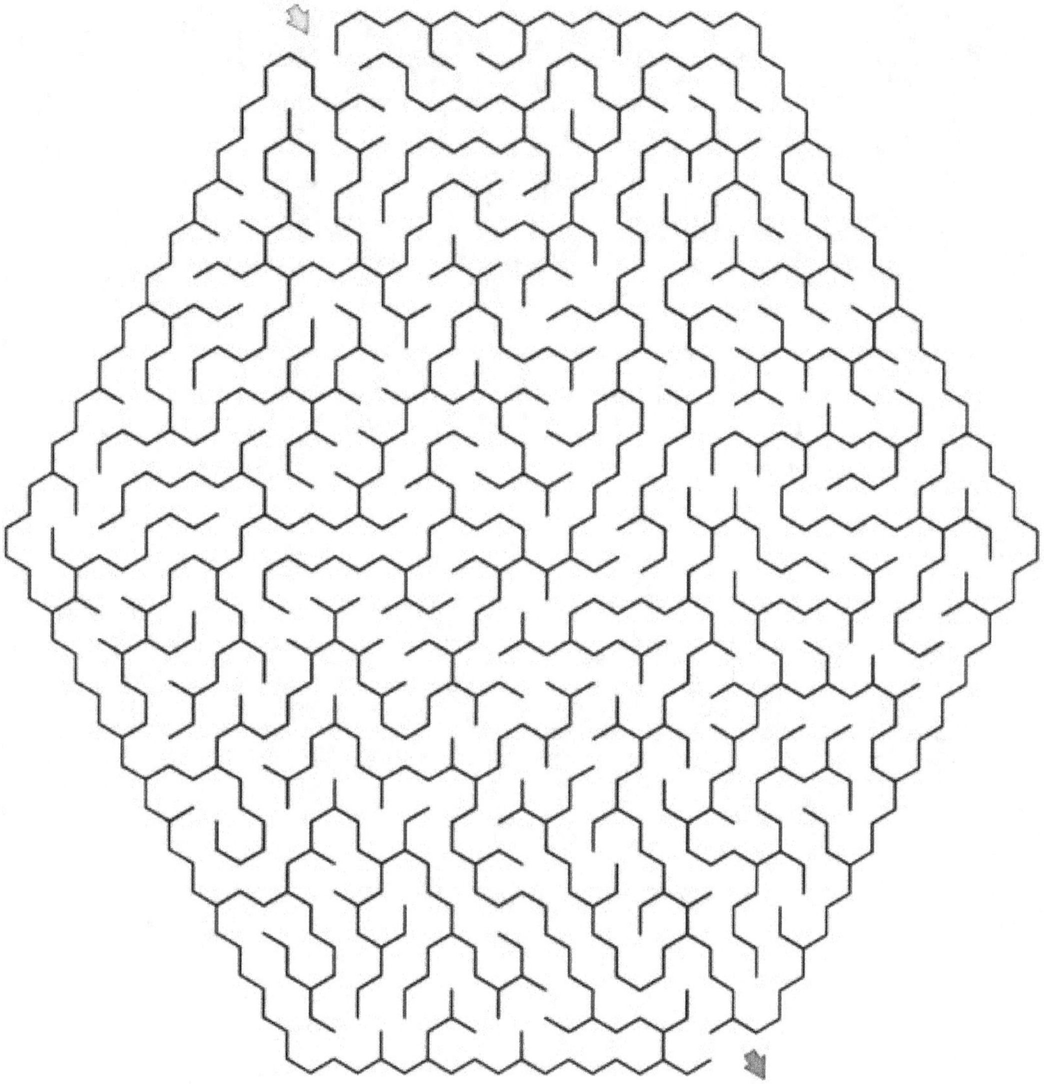

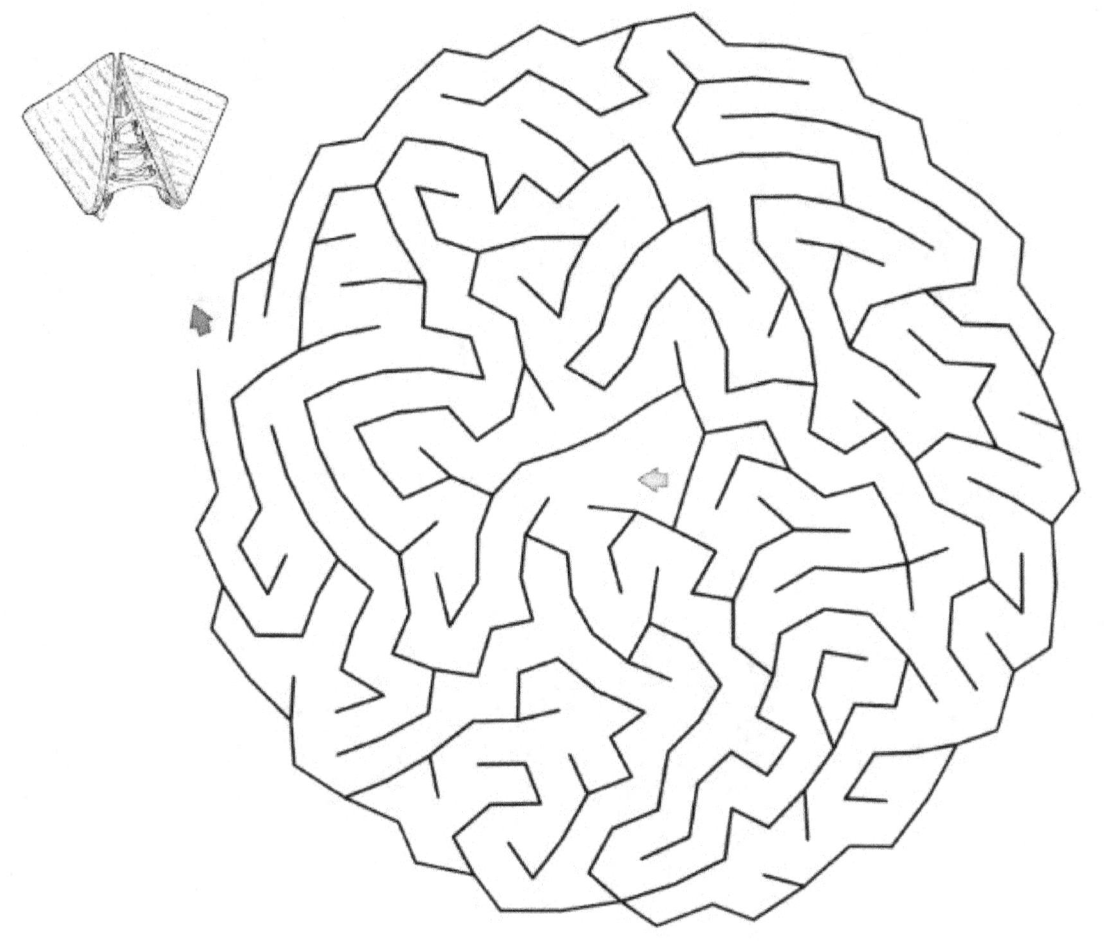

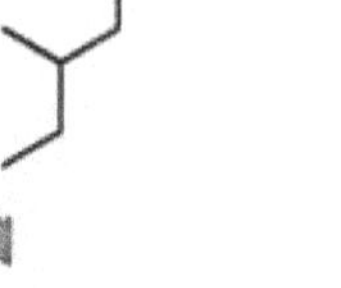

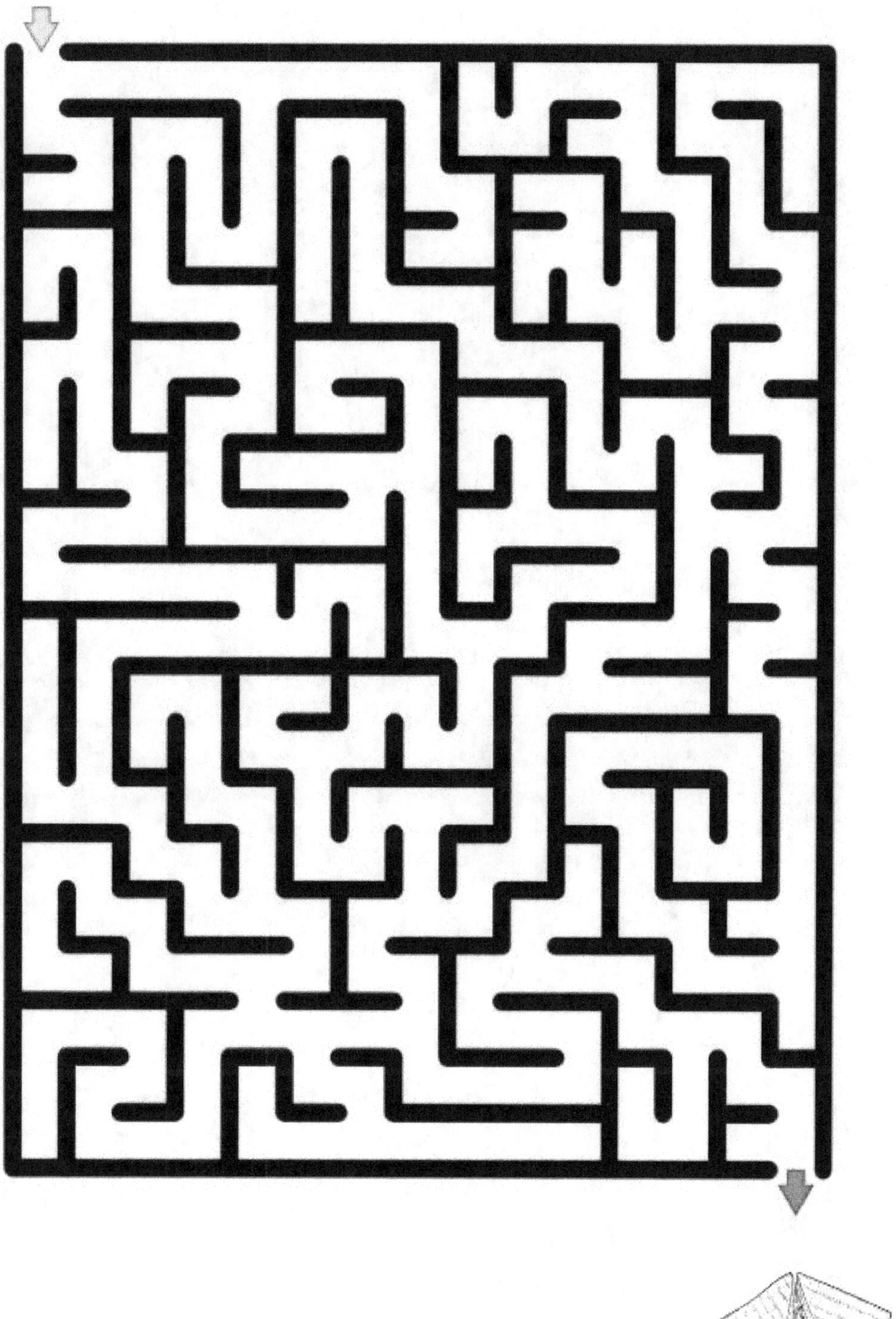

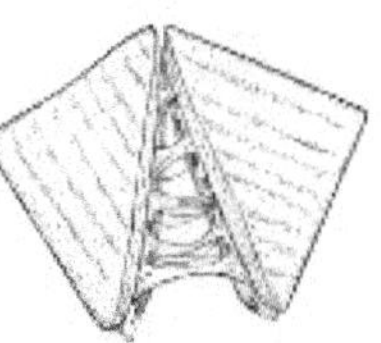

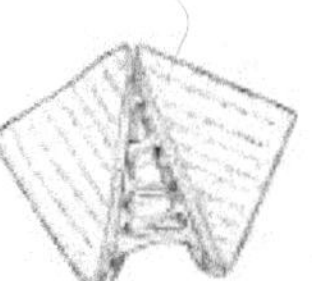

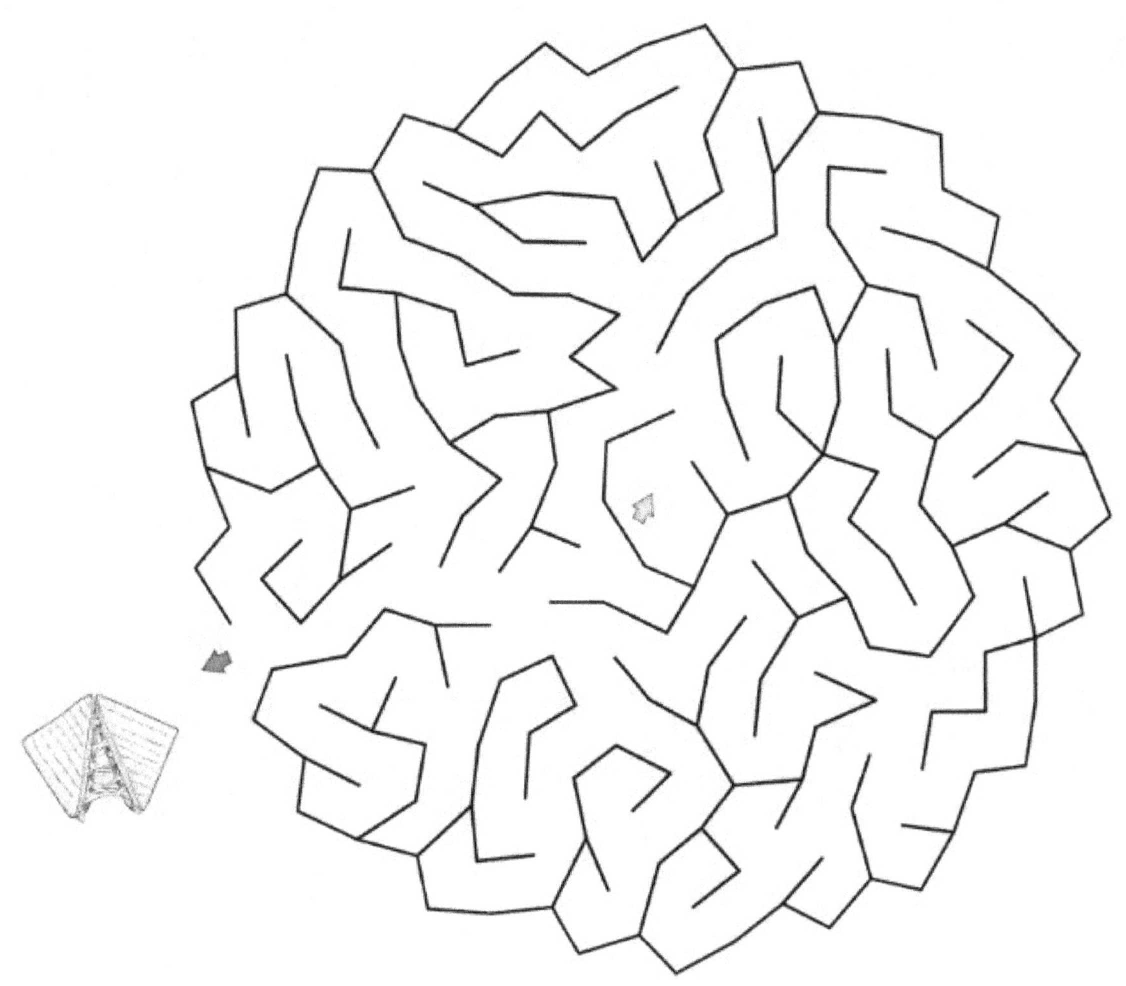

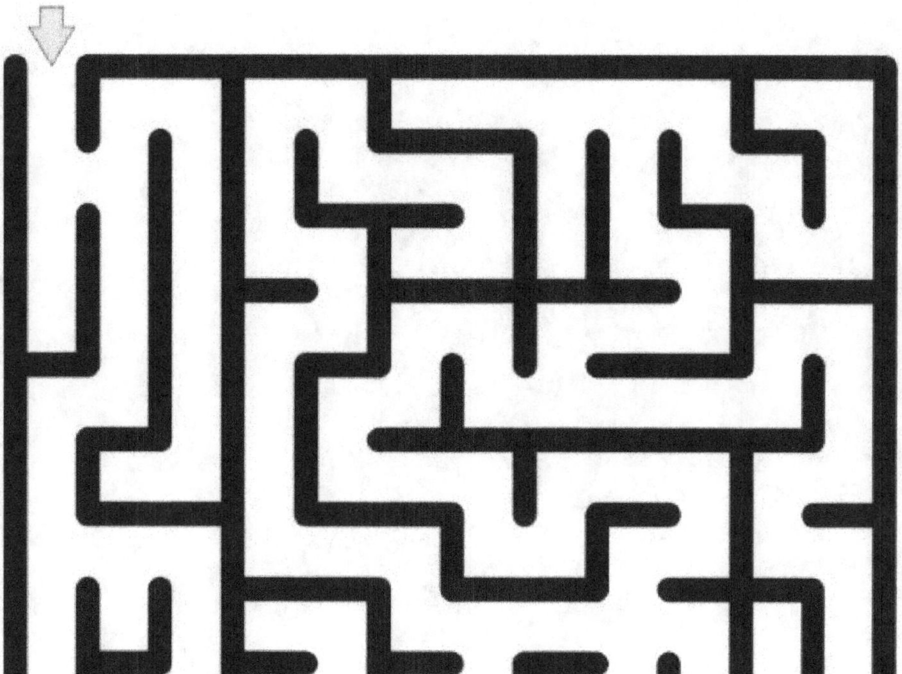

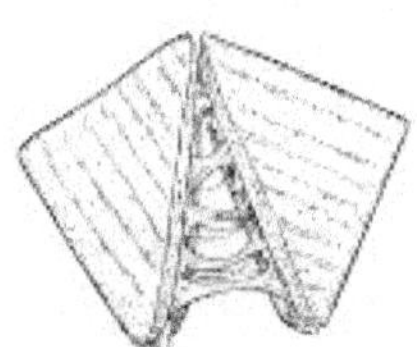

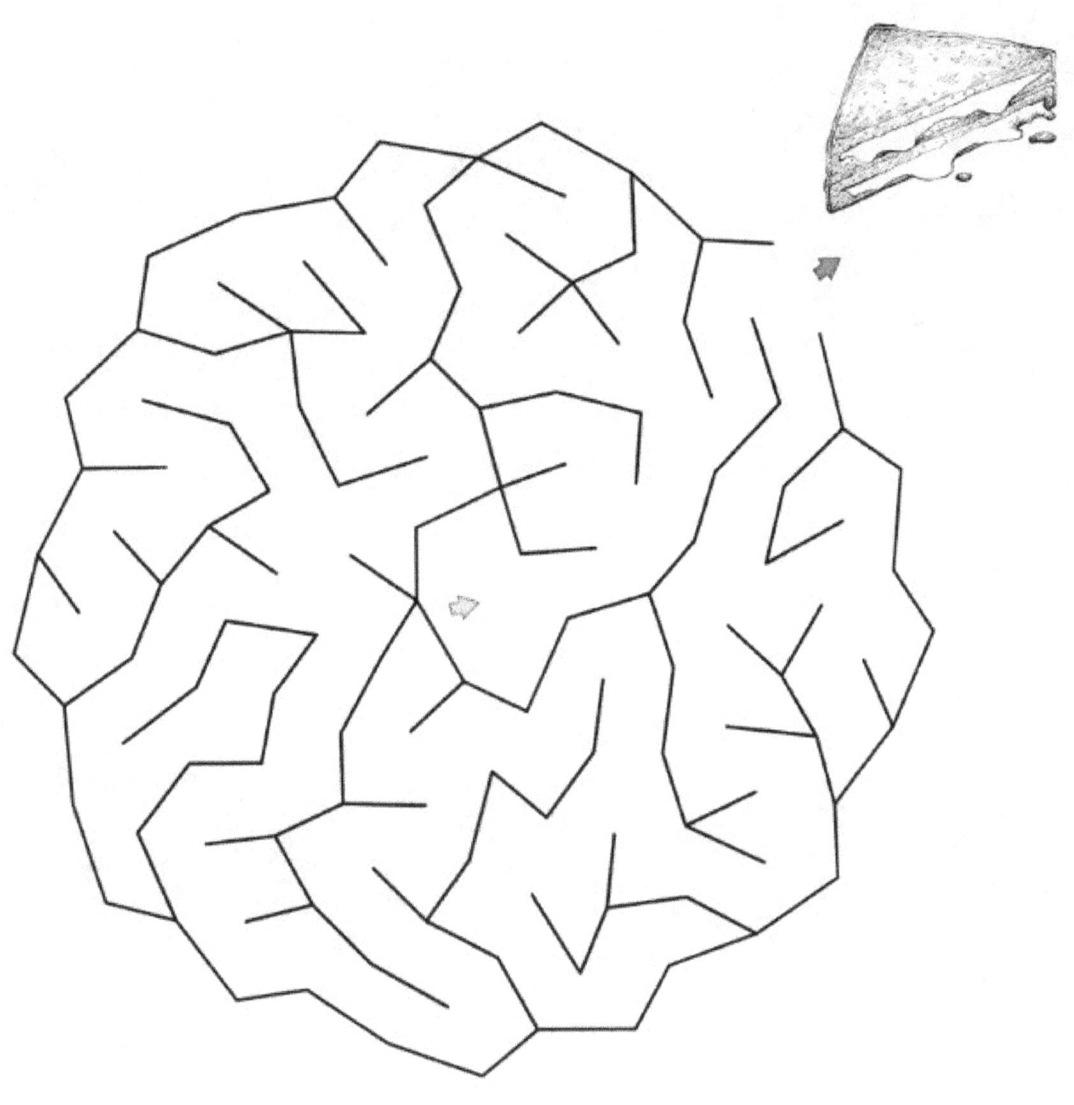

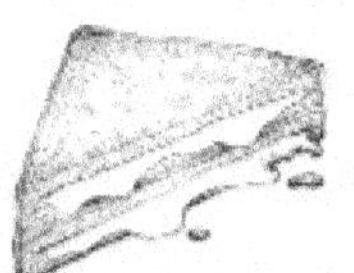

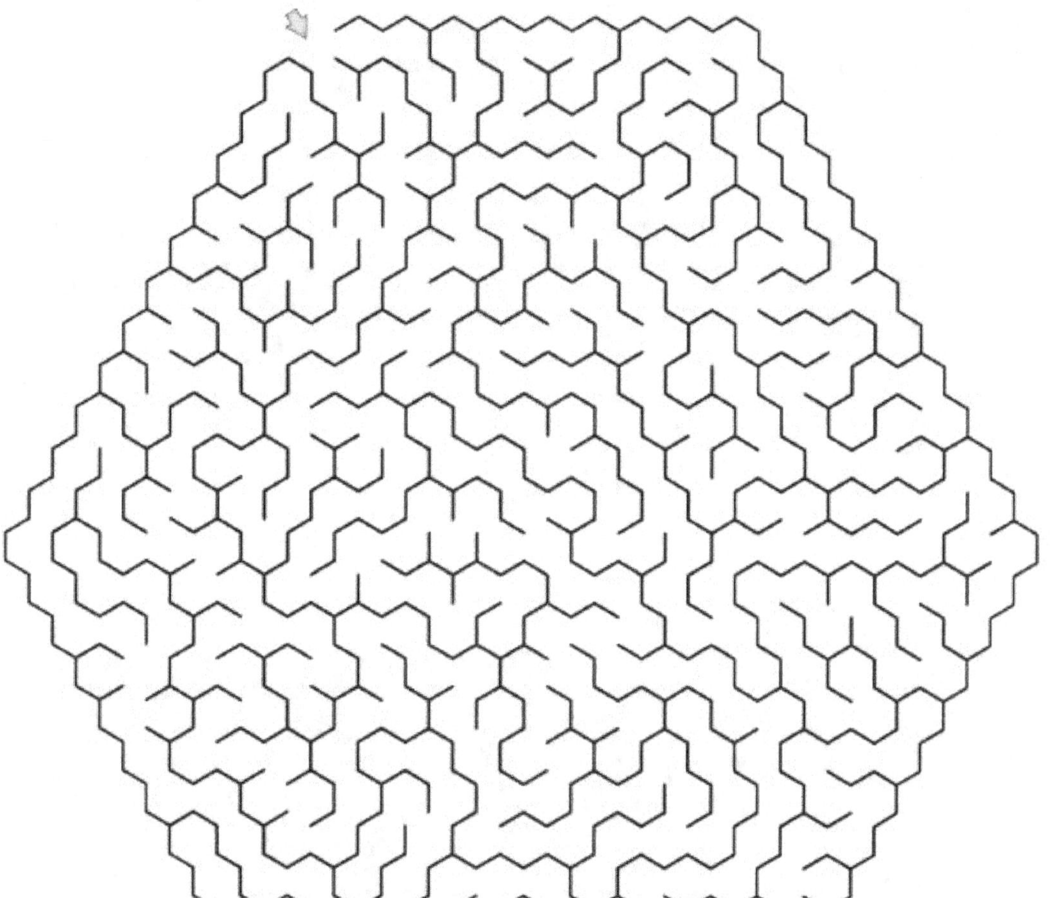

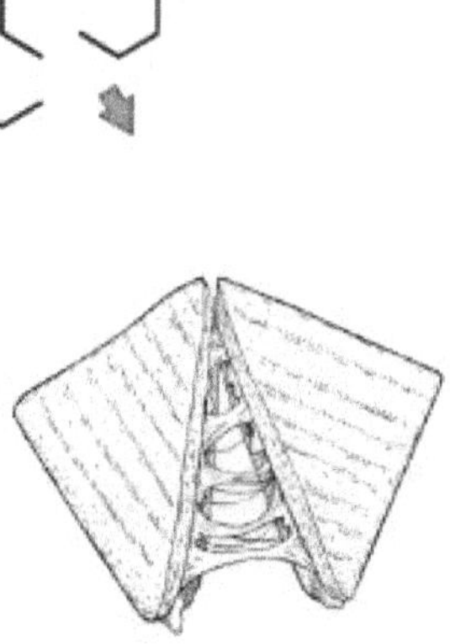

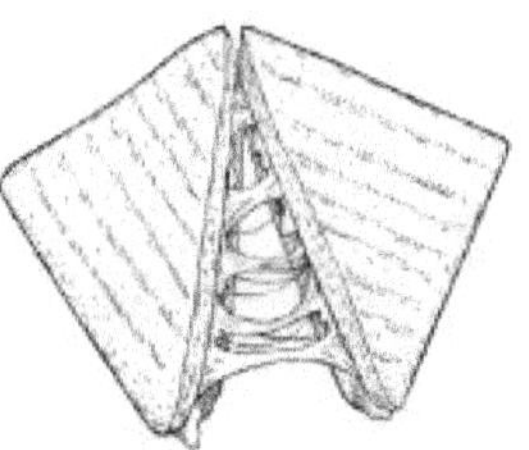

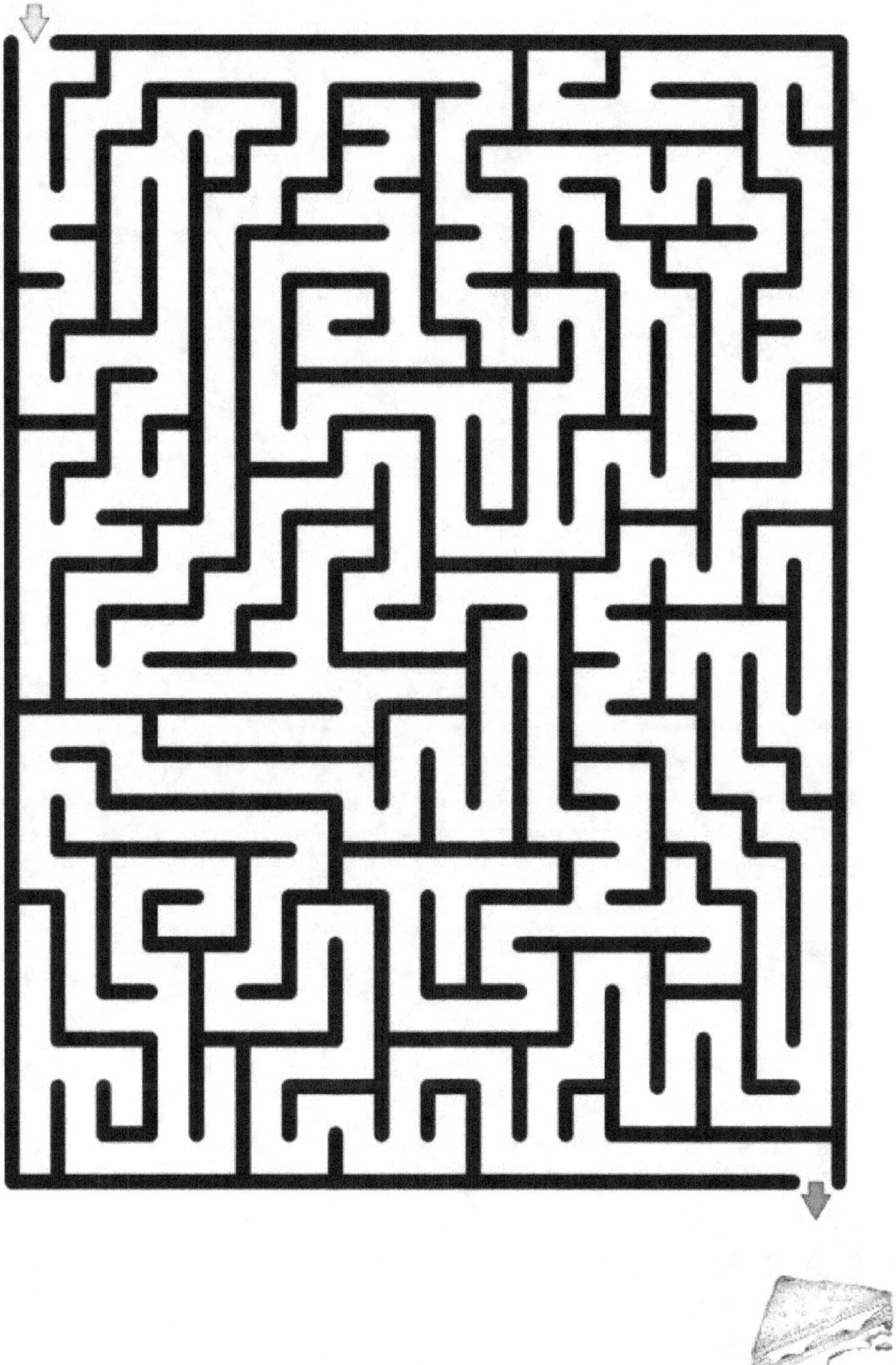

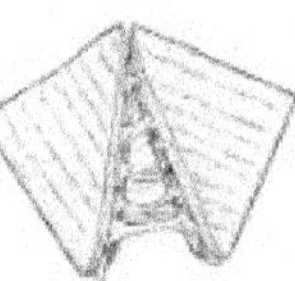

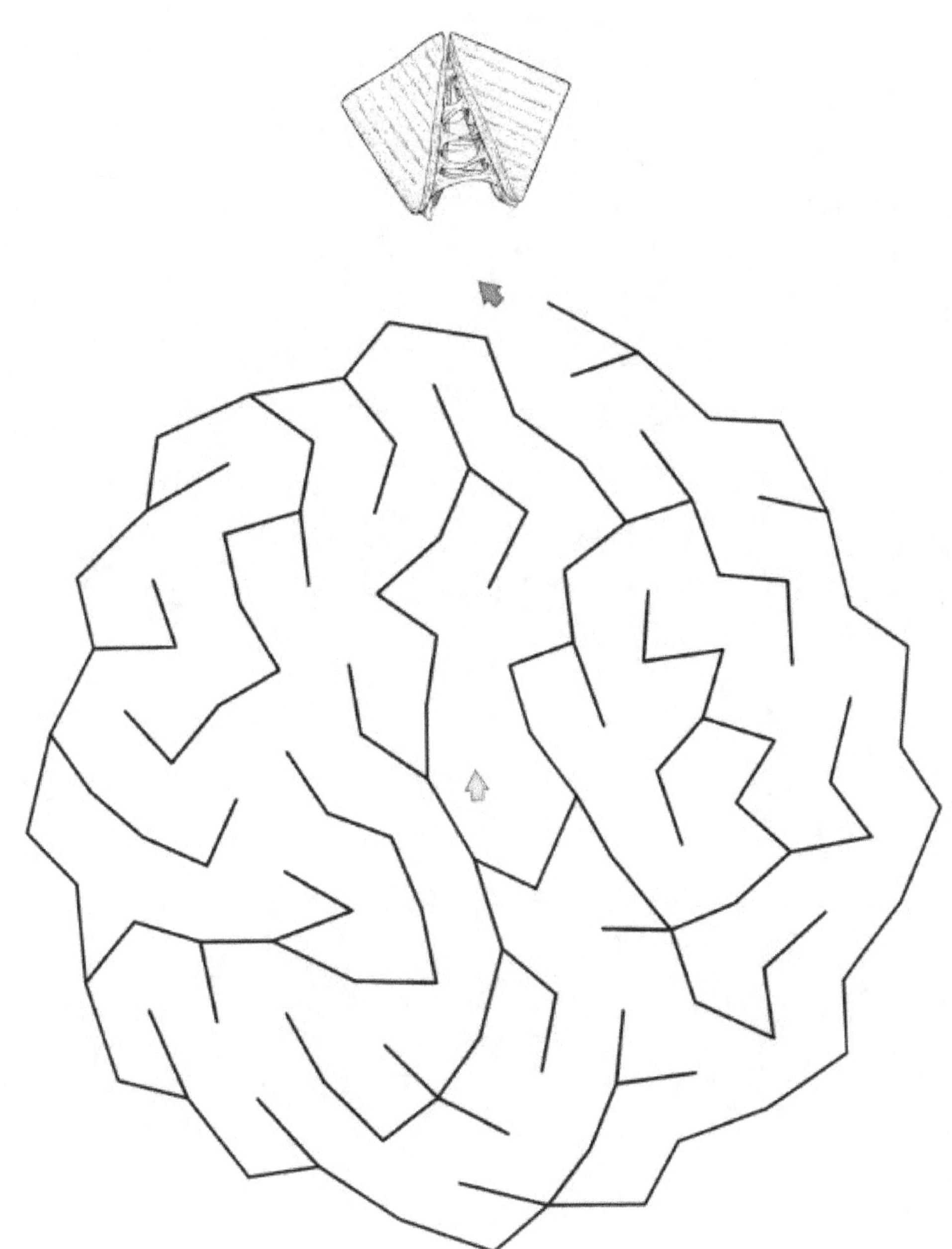

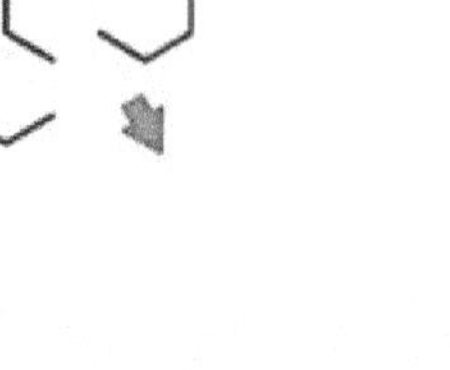

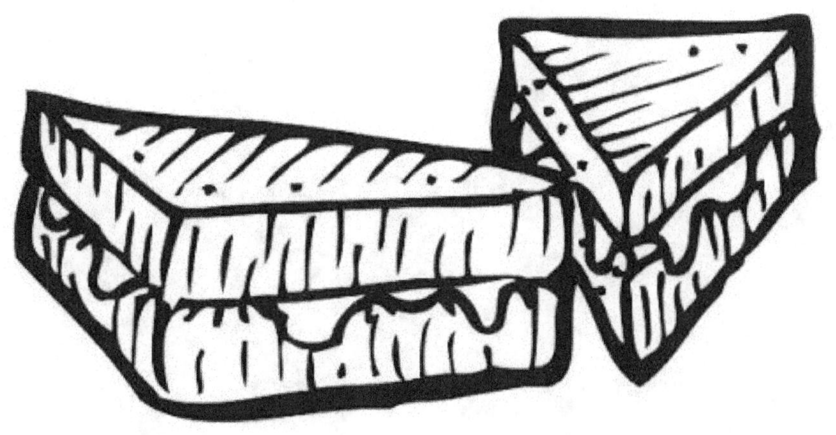